Insight of DeepMind Learning

Journey of transformation from Natural Intelligence to Artificial Intelligence

Md. Sadique Shaikh

ELIVA PRESS

ELIVA PRESS

Md. Sadique Shaikh

Deep reinforcement learning has rapidly become one of the hottest research areas in the deep learning ecosystem. The fascination with reinforcement learning is related to the fact that, from all the deep learning modalities, is the one that resemble the most how humans learn. In the last few years, no company in the world has done more to advance the stage of deep reinforcement learning than Alphabet's subsidiary DeepMind. Since the launch of its famous AlphaGo agent, DeepMind has been at the forefront of reinforcement learning research. A few days ago, they published a new research that attempts to tackle one of the most challenging aspects of reinforcement learning solutions: multi-tasking. Since we are infants, multi-tasking becomes an intrinsic element of our cognition. The ability to performing and learning similar tasks concurrently is essential to the development of the human mind. From the neuroscientific standpoint, multi-tasking remains largely a mystery and that, not surprisingly, we have had a heck of hard time implementing artificial intelligence (AI) agents that can efficiently learn multiple domains without requiring a disproportional amount of resources. This challenge is even more evident in the case of deep reinforcement learning models that are based on trial and error exercises which can easily cross the boundaries of a single domain. Biologically speaking, you can argue that all learning is a multi-tasking exercise. This monograph introduces you with DeepMind learning.

Published by Eliva Press SRL
Address: MD-2060, bd.Cuza-Voda, 1/4, of. 21 Chişinău, Republica
Moldova
Email: info@elivapress.com
Website: www.elivapress.com

ISBN: 978-1-63648-066-4

Insight of DeepMind Learning

Journey of transformation from Natural Intelligence to Artificial Intelligence....

Prof. Md. Sadique Shaikh

B.Sc. (ES), M.Sc. (ES), M.Tech. (IT),

D.B.M, P.G.D.M. (EM), M.B.A. (HRM),

M.B.A. (MM), M.Phil. , DMS (IBM), Ph.D.

AIMSR

Jalgaon, M.S, India

Dedicated to……..

My Mother **"Shahenaaz Parvin"**

My Wife **"Safeena Sadique Shaikh"**

My loving Son **"Md. Nameer Shaikh"**

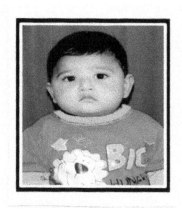

My loving Son **"Md. Shadaan Shaikh"**

My Close Friends **"Tanveer Sayyed"**

Content

Chapter One: Evolution of DeepMind learning

DeepMind learning as opposed to the wider fields of machine learning and artificial intelligence (AI) for four reasons. First, the vast majority of AI breakthroughs in recent years are *thanks to* deep learning. Second, deep learning is not a specific breakthrough; instead, it is a broadly applicable AI technique that is advancing the state of the art. Third, the technology industry is rallying around deep learning because of its step-function increase in performance and broad-based applications. Google, Facebook, Baidu, Microsoft, NVIDIA, Intel, IBM, Open AI, and various startups have made deep learning a central focus. Fourth, from an investor perspective, deep learning is only five years old and particularly compelling given its low revenue base, large addressable market, and high growth rate.

THE ORIGINS OF DEEP LEARNING

Deep learning is a modern name for an old technology—artificial neural networks. An artificial neural network, or simply neural net, is a computer program loosely inspired by the structure of the biological brain. The brain is made up of billions of cells called neurons connected via pathways called synapses. New observations and experiences alter the strength of the synaptic connections. Through the accumulation of observations and experience, the strength of the connections converges, resulting in "learning". Neural nets simulate these structures in software, with digital versions of neurons, synapses, and connection strengths. By feeding training examples, or "experience", to an artificial neural network and adjusting the weights accordingly, a neural net learns complex functions much like a biological brain.

The first neural network built on these biological principles was the Perceptron.1 This simple network used two layers of connected neurons and could be taught to perform simple image recognition tasks. Improved understanding of the visual cortex (the portion of the brain devoted to visual processing) led to the development of the Neocognitron, 2 a neural net composed of stacks of smaller, simpler layers. The use of multiple layers makes the network "deep" and allows it to perceive the world across multiple levels of abstraction. As a result, the Neocognitron was able to recognize characters in different positions and of various sizes.

Deep networks excelled at certain perception tasks, but they were difficult to train. In response, computer scientists developed backpropagation,3 a technique that trains deep networks by applying calculus to labeled data sets.

The combination of deep neural networks and back propagation yielded powerful results. In the early 1990s, a team led by Yann LeCun at AT&T Bell Labs developed a convolution neural network trained by back propagation that was able to read handwritten numbers with 99% accuracy at a 9% rejection rate.4 Subsequently, this system found its way into the banking system and processed more than 10% of all the checks in the United States.

Despite the early success of neural nets, the broader AI community was skeptical. Researchers generally preferred other machine learning algorithms that were simpler to implement, easier to train, and computationally less demanding. They favored Support Vector Machines, which performed on par with neural nets, for vision tasks in the 1990s.5 For voice recognition applications, they preferred hidden Markov models.

DEEP LEARNING TIMELINE

1958
Rosenblatt invents the "Perceptron", a machine that can detect shapes through a network of neuron-like hardware units.

1978
Fukushima invents "Neocognitron", a multi-layer neural network capable of detecting different shapes without being affected by shift position or minor distortion. This is the first convolutional neural network and the first "deep" architecture in the modern sense.

1986
Rumelhart, Hinton, and Williams popularizes "backpropagation" as an effective way to train deep neural nets. Backpropagation is the key breakthrough that makes neural nets effective learners and remains the dominant way neural nets are trained as of 2017.

1989
LeCun uses backpropagation to train convolutional neural nets and shows that the resulting network can read handwritten digits with 99% accuracy. This system is later widely deployed in ATMs for automated check reading.

2011
Google Brain, a deep neural network powered by 16,000 CPUs, learns to recognize cats by watching YouTube videos.

2011
Deep neural nets trained GPUs achieve 99% accuracy in street sign recognition, exceeding human performance for the first time in a controlled test.

2012
Deep neural net achieves record performance in classification of natural photographs in the ImageNet 2012 challenge, reducing error rates by 36% relative to existing machine learning programs. Neural nets go on to win the ImageNet contest in each of the next four years. This is considered by many to be the watershed moment in deep learning.

2013
Deep learning achieves record performance in a number of speech and character recognition tests.

2014
Facebook launches DeepFace, a deep neural net that detects faces with 97% accuracy, approaching human performance.

2015   Microsoft's ResNet deep neural net achieves 96% in the ImageNet classification challenge, reaching human level performance for the first time.

2015   Baidu Deep Speech 2 achieves human level performance in certain voice to text transcription for English and Mandarin in various benchmarks.

2016   DeepMind's AlphaGo, an AI program that combines deep learning with Monte Carlo tree search, defeats 18 time international champion Lee Sedol in the game of Go, reaching a major AI milestone ten years ahead of schedule.

THE RISE OF DEEP LEARNING

In 2012, neural networks began to deliver astounding performance results that far eclipsed other machine learning algorithms in both visual and audio applications. In image classification, deep learning reduced error rates from 26% to 3%. In voice recognition, deep learning reduced error rates from 16% to 6%. Critically, within the last two to three years, deep learning has surpassed human performance.

Deep learning has proven so effective that it has become core to the evolution of the technology industry. Google, Facebook, Microsoft, Apple, Baidu, IBM, and others have gravitated to deep learning for image and voice recognition. Likewise, AI startups like DeepMind, Vicarious, Nervana, OpenAI, Clarifai, and Enlitic, among others have focused on deep learning as their key enabling technology. The fact that companies large and small have embraced the same technology indicates that deep learning truly is distinguished relative to other machine learning algorithms, and explains why it has become foundational for next generation applications.

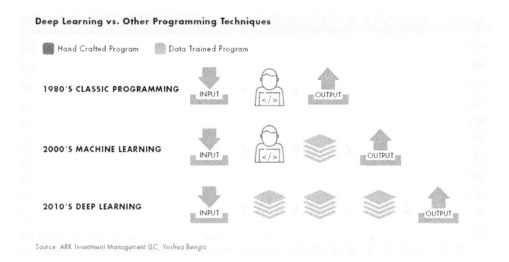

Deep Learning vs. Other Programming Techniques

■ Hand Crafted Program   ▒ Data Trained Program

1980'S CLASSIC PROGRAMMING — INPUT → OUTPUT

2000'S MACHINE LEARNING — INPUT → OUTPUT

2010'S DEEP LEARNING — INPUT → OUTPUT

Source: ARK Investment Management LLC, Yoshua Bengio

What makes deep learning unique is that it uses data to automate the programming process end-to-end, as shown above. In classic programming, humans manually design all parts of the program. This works for simple, well-defined problems but breaks down for more complex tasks. Machine learning improves upon this by replacing some stages of the program with stages that can be trained automatically with data, making it possible for computers to perform more complex tasks such as image and voice recognition.

Deep learning takes this idea to its logical conclusion and replaces the entire program with stages that can be trained with data. The result is that programs can be far more capable and accurate while requiring less human effort to create.

THE THREE DRIVERS OF GROWTH

According to ARK's research, three factors have contributed to the recent breakthroughs in deep learning: faster processor performance, larger data sets, and more sophisticated neural nets. In the charts below, we quantify how each of these factors has improved since the 1990s.

Processor performance has improved roughly five orders of magnitude since Intel's original Pentium processor for two reasons. First, thanks to 23 years of Moore's Law, the size of transistors has collapsed from 800nm to 16nm,6 enabling the creation of processors with billions of transistors operating in the gigahertz range and increasing computational power by five orders of magnitude. Second, graphics processing units (GPUs) emerged as a new class of microprocessors with roughly 10x the performance of central processing units (CPUs) when applied to the types of massively parallel operations required for deep learning.7 Consequently, a single processor today can perform over ten trillion calculations per second, making it possible to train highly complex neural networks in a matter of days. During the 1990s, the same computation would have taken multiple lifetimes.

The performance of deep learning programs is correlated highly to the amount of data used for training. While the performance of other machine learning algorithms plateau with more data, those associated with deep learning continue to scale with more training data, as shown below. Thanks to the internet's size and scale, deep learning has thrived with access to very large datasets at a minimal cost.

While LeCun's 1990 handwriting reader used approximately 10,000 samples collected from the US Postal Service, in 2009 ImageNet's dataset contained more than 10 million examples of high resolution photographs. Likewise, Baidu's DeepSpeech 28 draws upon over 10,000 hours of audio data compared to a few hundred hours in legacy data sets.

Chapter Two: Introduction to DeepMind Learning

Introduction

Machine learning can spot cancer. It can translate complex texts. Drive cars. Beat the best human in the world at one of the most complex games ever invented. Devise alien-like designs to create more efficient physical structures. Save energy. The science fiction writer and futurist Arthur C. Clarke wrote, "Any sufficiently advanced technology is indistinguishable from magic."1 The accomplishments above can indeed at times seem magical, but they are not. These successes are the result of a combination of innovative algorithms, powerful computers, and rich data. This mixture of algorithms, computers, and data can also, when misapplied or when misconfigured, make significant mistakes with catastrophic consequences. To see machine learning as sorcery rather than as a powerful tool that must be wielded carefully and thoughtfully is to invite enormous risk. Machine learning can also seem magical in another way: it can appear impossible to grasp. Our foundational premise in this paper is that this idea is false and dangerous. For each of the aforementioned achievements, and for several others, we will outline the concepts at play in a way that is accessible to generalists. Not only do we believe it is possible for non-specialists to gain intuition about how machine learning works, we think it is urgent. Several important principles are fundamental to understanding the power of machine learning, the opportunities it offers, and the new policy issues it raises. We proceed as follows. The first section outlines the basics of how machine learning works. It provides some important background on artificial intelligence, and discusses three main types of machine learning algorithms. The second section considers the current state of affairs, identifying areas of great progress in machine learning and in the process distilling important foundational concepts. In so doing, we show the ways in which machine learning has already had an impact on a variety of challenges. Next, we turn to the future. The third section examines how machine learning will affect areas of great importance to policymakers. In particular, we focus on war-fighting, healthcare, and policing. The discussion of these three areas shows the breadth of the change still to come, and the need for policymaker engagement.

While there are sector-specific reasons for policymaker engagement on machine learning, there are also overarching ones. The fourth section examines the challenges that come with the technology. In particular, it articulates concerns about data availability, privacy, fairness, security, and economic impact that must be carefully managed. Each of these areas, if not addressed by technologists and policymakers, represents a way in which poorly designed or applied machine learning tools could cause real harm. We believe they all deserve significant attention. As such, our conclusion provides recommendations on how policymakers can begin to approach machine learning to best maximize its potential and overcome its dangers.

How Does Machine Learning Work

Machine learning is the process of instructing computers to learn. It exists at the intersection of computer science, statistics, and linear algebra, with insights from neuroscience and other fields as well. But unlike traditional software development, machine learning involves programming computers to teach themselves from data rather than instructing them to perform certain tasks in certain ways. Machine learning is traditionally focused on prediction and creating structure out of unstructured data. In early efforts at artificial intelligence, researchers would attempt to instruct computers to act based on clear preset rules with fixed conditions.

For example, a very basic spam filter program might be told to mark as spam every email with a subject that contains the full phrase "cheap imported drugs." This approach has the advantage of being straightforward, but it is also inflexible; spammers who instead use the subject "discounted imported drugs" can defeat the system. In contrast, a machine learning program forgoes these few predetermined rules, which are often too broad or too narrow to be effective. The modern machine learning program instead identifies on its own a large number of more subtle patterns and features in data given to it for training purposes. It then uses these insights to assess new data. When making an assessment, such as whether or not an email is spam, the machine learning program will evaluate all of the features of the new data and compare them to the patterns it has seen before.

For engineers, building a machine learning capability can often take a great deal of fine-tuning and experimentation, as well as the use of conceptually interesting techniques (some of which will be discussed below). In addition, many machine learning techniques require computing power that has only very recently become available to those outside of government, even though the concepts themselves are older. To simplify the enormous amount of complexity and variation in these systems, machine learning algorithms are often divided into three broad categories

Supervised learning, unsupervised learning, and *reinforcement learning.* Each of these is a different method of applying machines to a problem.

Supervised Learning

Supervised learning algorithms enable machines to make predictions or assessments; they are widely used in everyday life, from voice recognition to email spam filters to medical predictions. The "supervised" part of the name comes from the fact that each piece of data given to the algorithm also contains the correct answer about the characteristic of interest, such as whether an email is spam or not, so that the algorithm can learn from past data and test itself by making predictions. To do this, the computer is usually given three things:

• A set of data to learn from. The data can be provided in a table or spreadsheet format, but must be labeled with the correct categories.

• A model that determines how the computer approaches the problem of assessing the data, with parameters that fine-tune the model to make the predictions as accurate as possible. There are numerous machine learning models.

• The cost function that calculates the error, or how far the algorithm is from perfect performance.

A description of one supervised machine learning model, the support vector machine (SVM), can illustrate how machine learning works on a more technical level when applied to the problem of predicting whether an email is spam or not spam. Starting with a dataset of emails (represented as dots on the graph on the next page) labeled as spam or not spam, an SVM will try to find the line that best separates the two categories of data points, as seen below with the line dividing the blue and brown areas.3 The parameters in this case determine the location and curves of the line. The SVM distinguishes between the categories through an iterative process of starting with a random line, determining what changes to the line (made through parameter adjustments) decrease its error as calculated by the cost function. It then iteratively adjusts its parameters until the error is minimized to its fullest extent; at that point, the best separating line has been found. Once that line is found, new emails can be plotted on this graph and their category (blue or brown; spam or not spam) can be predicted from their relationship to this line.

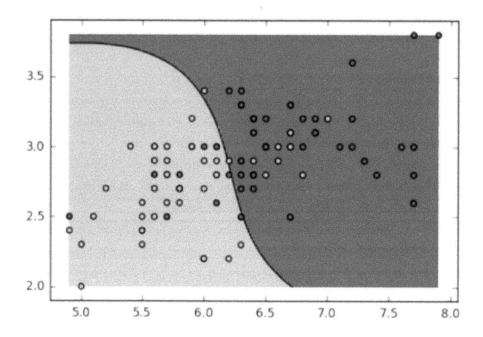

SVM is only one of numerous supervised learning models that are used, and a number of models take different approaches to the same problem.

The image on the next page shows how ten different supervised learning models divide the same set of data into two categories, red or blue; the shading indicates confidence intervals. Importantly, each algorithm has its strengths and weaknesses, and machine learning practitioners will often try a number of models to determine which one works best for the problem they are trying to solve.

A common analogy is that the supervised learning model is a box with thousands of adjustable knobs, which represent parameters, and the goal of supervised learning is to adjust the knobs to find the configuration that minimizes overall error. Adjusting the parameters allows the model to uncover the patterns in the data that are important for prediction. After the model finds the best parameter configuration, it can use this configuration to make predictions when given new data. In addition to support vector machines, there are a number of different types of supervised learning algorithms, such as decision trees, Bayesian networks, and more. The details of each of these are beyond the scope of this paper. More important is that, while these approaches are diverse in their applications and relative advantages, they all follow the same basic concept.

Unsupervised Learning

Supervised learning algorithms benefit from the guidance provided by the training set of data, and sometimes by real-time feedback about whether their predictions are correct. Sometimes data isn't so neatly structured, though. Unsupervised learning is more useful when there is not a clear outcome of interest about which to make a prediction or assessment. Unsupervised learning algorithms are given large amounts of data and try to identify key structures, or patterns, within them.

One common task for these algorithms is to spot clusters in a set of data. The clusters represent groups that each share meaningful characteristics. Clustering is very useful in market segmentation, for example. It can break data representing an undifferentiated sea of customers into groups that share preferences and interests, enabling companies to better tailor their products and marketing to each group. But a key insight bears repeating: in unsupervised learning, the algorithm finds the clusters on its own, and is not given any preconceived notions about how to break down the data into groups.

One unsupervised machine learning method, k-means, can help illustrate how unsupervised learning works. A company may want to perform market segmentation with the customer data shown in the image, dividing its customers into three segments for more accurate advertising or pricing.

The k-means algorithm would randomly propose three (or the desired number of clusters) points on the graph to be the centers of the new clusters. It would then adjust these center points iteratively in the direction that minimizes the distance between the center point and all of the points in its cluster, while also maximizing the distance between the center point and all points not in its cluster. The end product, as shown in the image, is three separate and well defined clusters, with customers matched to the cluster of the closest center point.

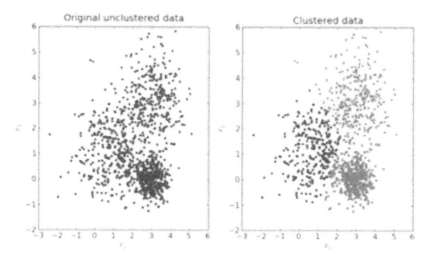

One of the most common uses of unsupervised learning is to better understand the structure of data in order to build better supervised learning algorithms. For example, unsupervised learning can be used to combine the multitude of pixels from a picture into a small number of important recognizable features. These features, such as the structures of the eyes, nose, and mouth can then serve as an input for a supervised learning facial\ recognition algorithm. Notice that the each of the three images below highlights facial features that would be important for identification—features derived through unsupervised learning.

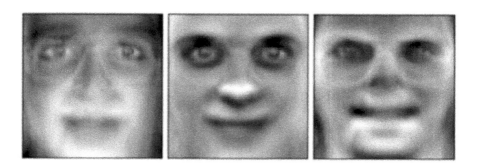

Reinforcement Learning

Rather than simply manipulating data, reinforcement learning algorithms work by introducing software known as a machine learning agent to an environment and teaching it how to act. Unsurprisingly, reinforcement learning is very important in robotics, though it's most public successes have been in defeating humans in games.

DeepMind, a leading artificial intelligence company that was purchased by Google in 2014, has been a pioneer in reinforcement learning. In 2015, they devised a program that would learn how to play basic video games.

The agent in this program got only the information on the screen, including the score of the game, and nothing else—not even the rules. It then proceeded to make decisions, randomly at first, and to see the rewards or failures of its choices. Over hundreds or sometimes thousands of iterations of the game, the agent saw which decisions, or series of decisions, led to better rewards in certain conditions. This information became the basis of its approach to playing the games well. The DeepMind game-playing agent was able to beat professional game players in more than three-fourths of the games it tried.

Reinforcement learning returned to the news in 2016 with perhaps its highest profile success. DeepMind applied reinforcement learning alongside deep learning (discussed below) to the ancient board game Go. Go is a game that had long been considered too difficult for artificial intelligence to master because of the many combinations of possible moves; there are many more possible Go board combinations than atoms in the universe, and many more combinations than in even other complex games like chess. Playing Go well is not just a matter of calculation, but of intuition— something at which machines are famously weaker than humans.

DeepMind's agent, named AlphaGo, observed many thousands of games of professional Go to understand the important patterns. It then began to play millions of games of Go against itself, refining its capabilities and uncovering additional insights. This highlights the immense scale made possible by machines; AlphaGo in a short period of time played more games of Go than even the most dedicated players can play in a lifetime. It used the insights from these games in a widely-publicized set of matches in 2016 and 2017 to defeat the top players in the world. In so doing, it introduced new ideas and strategies that had eluded players ever since the invention of the game.

The Current State of Machine Learning

An old joke goes something like this: "Once something works, we stop calling it artificial intelligence and start calling it software." Moving the goalposts of artificial intelligence, of which machine learning is a part, is a repeated pattern: as advances have continued, such as defeating humans in chess, then *Jeopardy!*, and then later in Go, we have been reluctant to recognize each step as artificial intelligence in and of itself. Instead, artificial intelligence is often viewed as something that is perpetually over the horizon. While there are many goals that are out of immediate reach, this perspective can obscure the progress that has already been made. By focusing on the ways in which machine learning has already been applied with success and looks poised to grow still further, this section draws out several important and overlapping concepts of critical importance.

The Importance of Data

While conceptual breakthroughs in the design of machine learning programs are significant, machine learning still relies on data. In a groundbreaking 2001 paper, Michele Banko and Eric Brill showed that the amount of data used to train machine learning algorithms has a greater effect on prediction accuracy than the type of machine learning method used; see the graph on the next page.10 In other words, for some problems, a decent algorithm that learns from a lot of relevant data outperforms a great algorithm that learns from minimal or poor data. This is one of the reasons why some of the most successful companies today are the ones that have the most data on which to train their programs, and why companies are willing to pay massive amounts of money for more data. As Peter Norvig, Google's Chief Scientist, once said, "We don't have better algorithms than anyone else; we just have more data."

The Deep Learning Approach

Deep learning is perhaps the most promising area of machine learning today. While supervised, unsupervised, and reinforcement learning are all overarching methods, deep learning is an architecture that can implement those methods; for example, deep reinforcement learning systems are quite powerful. Deep learning uses networks that contain layers of nodes that in some ways mimic the neurons in the brain. Each layer of neurons takes the data from the layer below it, performs a calculation, and provides its output to the layer above it. Deep learning can combine an unsupervised process to learn the features of the underlying data (such as the edge of a face) and then provide that information to a supervised learning algorithm to recognize features as well as the final result (correctly identifying the person in the picture). More generally speaking, deep learning is useful for capturing hierarchical meaning; for example, it can grasp from images that cats have body parts, and not the other way around, and that those body parts are made up of shapes. Deep learning is used today for everything from better understanding the molecular interactions inside human cells to improving computer vision and natural language processing.

Another area in which deep learning has yielded tangible benefits is in improving energy efficiency. For example, the operation of thousands of servers that drive any tech company creates a great deal of heat. As a result, cooling data centers is an enormous challenge and one that, if not managed well, can quickly become financially and environmentally costly. While Google had already made enormous efforts to increase its cooling efficiency—from 2011 to 2016, the company tripled how much computing power it got per unit of energy—machine learning enabled still greater progress.

DeepMind devised an approach that improved cooling efficiency in Google's data centers by 40 percent. The company trained neural networks with historical data from thousands of sensors to understand the complex interactions between equipment, operational decisions, and environmental factors such as weather. In so doing, the machine learning approach was able to identify subtle but substantial ways in which even a company as advanced as Google could improve. Google's graph provides visualization of how enabling the machine learning approach reduces power usage (as measured by a Google statistic known as PUE; lower is better).

In a world warming due to climate change and facing still growing energy demands, this example provides hope that machine learning could help meet energy needs through increased efficiency.

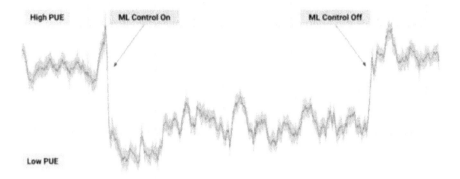

High PUE   ML Control On   ML Control Off

Low PUE

Progress in Computer Vision

Machine learning enables computers to identify objects in pictures. This skill can be used to make predictions that exceed human accuracy. As outlined earlier, to achieve computer vision, the first layer of a deep learning program is given the data from individual pixels in an image, and it learns which characteristics are most important. At the lowest levels of the process, the characteristics or features identified are as simple as finding the edge of an object. The features are progressively passed up to higher layers in the network, where more complex features are learned. The final layer then uses these features to identify the objects in the picture.

This capacity for computer vision has a wide range of applications, most notably in medicine. For example, it is often difficult to develop accurate prognoses for lung cancer patients. Using several thousand images, however, a machine learning algorithm was able to examine many detailed and nuanced characteristics of the cancers. This went beyond size and shape of cell to include things like spatial relationships between cells and the texture and shape of cell nuclei. While human experts regularly examine several hundred characteristics of cancer cells in order to make a prognosis, machine algorithms were able to examine nearly ten thousand characteristics and determine which were most important. As one investigator noted, "the computers can assess even tiny differences across thousands of samples many times more accurately and rapidly than a human." The result is better assessment of patients' conditions and better understanding of the progression of cancer; other examples of deep learning algorithms can aid pathologists and reduce human errors by 85 percent.

Improvements in Natural Language Processing

One common aspiration, imagined in a plethora of science fiction works, is a computer that can read, listen, understand, translate, and talk. Formally, this kind of work is known as natural language processing. Machine learning has enabled significant advances in this area. Google Brain, a machine learning division of the company that focuses on applications to Google products, had enormous success in improving the quality of translations when it deployed a neural network-based approach. In one of its early deployments, the machine learning algorithm was able to improve Google Translate's French BLEU score—a key metric for evaluating translation quality—by seven points. Previously, improvements of one and two points were considered impressive.16

More work remains to be done on natural language processing. Andrew Ng, the founder of Google Brain and the former Chief Scientist at Baidu, estimates that computers can recognize about 95% of speech in 2017.17 Ng believes that while the rate of mistakes is reasonably low, it is still significant enough to pose a substantial hurdle in interactions; he thinks the difference between 95% and 99% accuracy is the difference between talking to computers sporadically as we do today and seamlessly talking to computers without thinking anything of it.18 There are many challenges in this area, such as getting computers to understand ideas rather than just transcribe or act on them. If those problems are solved, the nature of human interaction with machines will be very different.

The Ever-Increasing Internet of Things

The growth in machine learning intersects with massive growth in other areas. Perhaps chief among these is the Internet of Things—interconnected devices of all types, from thermostats to toasters. Machine learning provides the potential to allow each device to learn its user's personal preferences and proactively get better at its task. For example, each

Nest-branded thermostat gathers information about its user's habits and temperature preferences, and eventually learns to set the temperature to optimal levels itself, based on a variety of factors. This can result in gains in not just comfort, but also energy efficiency.

Toasters and thermostats may, in the scheme of life, be of reasonably low significance compared to near-future Internet of Things devices. Self-driving cars, for example, will use machine learning to stay on the road, but also to customize themselves to their various users or to best predict which route is fastest. A wide range of companies will employ machine learning in their equipment, sometimes referred to as the Industrial Internet of Things. Some of this equipment, such as the software and hardware that makes up the industrial control networks of critical infrastructure, serves vitally important societal functions. While there are no doubt enormous gains in efficiency to come from the convergence of the Internet of Things and machine learning, there is also no doubt about the stakes. In situations like these, machine learning algorithms must perform exceptionally well or risk dangerous consequences.

Changing Approach to Design

What enables machine learning algorithms to achieve better results on some problems? It is not a question of machines being "smart" or humans being "dumb." Instead, improvements are often driven by machines' ability to execute a large number of calculations and better account for enormous amounts of data. More provocative, perhaps, is the idea that machines are not wedded to conventional notions. Instead, they will consider (and sometimes use) approaches that are counterintuitive but superior. Taken together, the ability to consider many possibilities and the capacity to be free of preconceived notions is powerful.19 It also results in some solutions that seem alien in nature, even though they work quite well. For example, the image below shows how a generative design algorithm—a computer- driven approach to design—devised an unconventional load-bearing column that uses vastly less material but is equally effective. This capacity for efficient design holds enormous promise in areas like manufacturing.

The Transformational Effects of Machine Learning

Andrew Ng, the aforementioned research scientist formerly of Google Brain and Baidu, provides a useful heuristic for understanding where machine learning is today: "If a typical person can do a mental task with less than one second of thought, we can probably automate it using AI either now or in the near future."21 He has called AI "the new electricity," in that it at some point will be ubiquitous and will fundamentally reshape how humans live and societies function.22 While the previous section showed how machine learning has already made substantial improvements in a range of areas, this section highlights the ways in which machine learning, now and especially in the future, will present new opportunities and challenges in particular areas vital for policymakers.

Before that, however, it is worth reflecting on the limits of machine learning. These, in some ways, can be counterintuitive: machine learning algorithms get better at some tasks much faster than they get better at others. This is often the case even if other types of non-machine learning software perform differently, even if humans learn both tasks at the same speed, and even if humans think that both tasks are equally part of "intelligence." For example, machine learning algorithms are often much better at recognizing parts of images than they are recognizing how words relate to concepts. They are also, as a generalization, much worse at learning when they have less data on which to rely; large amounts of data often overwhelm humans, but often have a positive, rather than negative, effect on machine learning algorithms' performance. Similarly, while humans are very good at quickly transferring ideas from one context to another, machines sometimes struggle with this.

As we consider how machine learning affects specific disciplines, we have tried to highlight the tasks in those disciplines in which algorithms are likely to be very effective and impactful, but it is worth remembering that algorithms will not be universally so.

Chapter Three: DeepMind Learning Machine research in progress

Artificial intelligence, machine learning and deep learning

Artificial intelligence, machine learning and deep learning are terms that are often used as synonyms even though they are conceptually imprecise. The illustration depicts the relationship between the terms and their development over time.

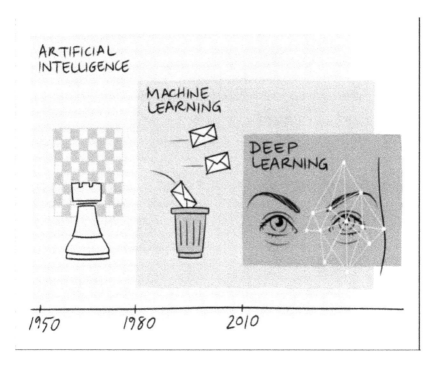

Artificial intelligence is an umbrella term that embraces many different types of machine learning. Machine learning can be described as "a set of techniques and tools that allow computers to 'think' by creating mathematical algorithms based on accumulated data".5 The system can reason independently of human input, and can itself build new algorithms.

Deep learning is a form of machine learning. Some types of deep learning build on the same principles as the brain's neural network. Systems of this type are often based on a known set of training data that helps the self-learning algorithms to carry out a task. This is conditional on the network itself being able to determine the correct response for solving the task.6 This method was crucial in enabling the AlphaGo computer program to defeat one of the world's best players of the Chinese board game Go (see fact box). This was considered to be an important milestone in the continuing development of AI.

Machine learning

In order to understand why AI needs huge volumes of data, it is necessary to understand how the system learns.

Developing AI requires the input of experiential data. Machine learning generally proceeds in this way: (Illustrated by Figure 1, *from left to right*):

1. Learning starts with selected information containing patterns or similarities.

2. By using machine learning, the patterns found in the information are identified.

3. A model is generated that can recognise the patterns that emerge when fresh data is processed by the model.

Model is an umbrella term for the final outcome of learning. There are many different types of models and it is these that are used in commercial applications — such as predicting the type of streamed TV series a consumer prefers. What these models have in common is that they contain essential training data. As the data that the model will process in the future will seldom be completely identical with the training data, a generalisation is required. Certain data that deviate from the main bulk of training data, will therefore usually be removed from the model.

This is how the model works: (Illustrated by Figure 1, *from top to bottom*)

1. The model receives data similar to that used for learning.

2. The model decides which pattern the new data most resembles.

3. The model produces an estimated result.

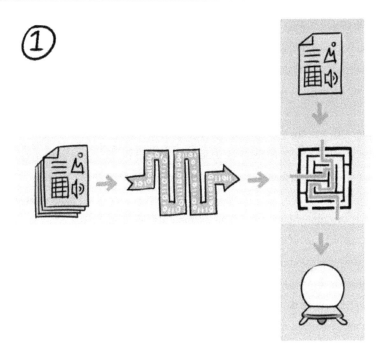

There are several forms of learning that can be used, depending on whether the information has been labelled or not. Labelled data is tagged data: if the data consists of images, the labels or tags may for example be gender, ethnicity, dog or cat.

Below we have listed the main forms of learning, and we describe how the data is used in these.

Supervised learning

Supervised learning involves the use of labelled data, by means of which the supervision is performed. The dataset is split into two, usually an 80/20 split, with 80 per cent of the data used to train the model. The remaining 20 per cent is used to verify how precisely the model processes unknown data. It is no good if the model performs accurately using the training data and inaccurately using new and unknown data. If the model is too well adjusted to the training data, which we call overfitting, it will not produce satisfactory results using new data. Therefore, the model requires a certain degree of generalisation.

Training data may for example consist of images labelled with information about the contents of each image. Supervised learning may be compared to teaching a child. For example, we point to a number of objects to the child and give them names. If we show a number of cats to a child, the child will gradually learn to recognise other cats than those originally shown. In similar fashion, a machine learning model will develop the same ability to recognise objects based on labelled images.

If one is working with a dataset and wishes to separate men and women, one can use different features that are of relevance. The features used will depend on the basic data available. For example, women live longer than men on average, so life duration is of relevance when differentiating between genders. This feature will, however, prove to be somewhat narrow in most cases, and is mentioned here only as an example. If one's data basis consists of images, then hair length, or the use of make-up or jewellery, may be relevant features. The example below illustrates how two different features are used in learning.

Learning takes place as follows (Illustrated by figure 2, *from left to right*):

1. A set of labelled data is used.

2. Depending on data type, and what is considered relevant, the features (circles and triangles) to be used for learning are selected. The data is labelled to denote the right answer.

3. A model is built that, based on the same features, will produce a label.

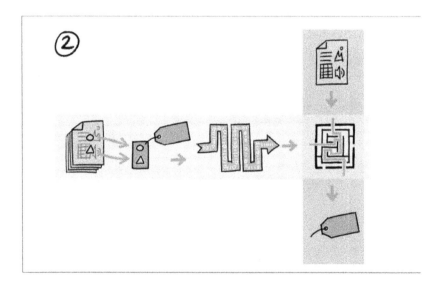

We will often also know which features of labelled data are most decisive for correct categorisation or for producing the right result. It is important to have persons with sound knowledge of the field in question in order to identify the most relevant features. The correct selection of relevant features may be of much more importance than the amount of data, an issue we will be addressing later. One advantage of labelled data is that it enables an easy check of the model's precision.

When we use the model, the following takes place (Fig. 2, *top to bottom*):

1. New data of the same type as the training data is fed into the system.

2. The relevant features are fed into the model and processed.

3. The model produces a result that corresponds with the labels used in training.

Unsupervised learning

In unsupervised learning, data is used that has not been pre-labelled, as the aim is for the system to group data that is similar. If, for the sake of simplicity, we again consider data consisting of cat and dog images, the goal would be for this data, to the greatest extent possible, to be sorted into two groups – one consisting of images of dogs, and the other of cat images.

Learning proceeds as follows (Fig.3, *left to right*):

1. A dataset is used in which there must be a certain number of similarities, or patterns, if it is to be meaningful.

2. The patterns are revealed.

3. A model is built that can recognise and differentiate patterns.

This is what takes place when using the model (Fig. 3, *top to bottom*):

1. New unlabelled data of the same type as the training data is fed into the system.

2. The model identifies the data patterns.

3. The model tells which group the new data belongs to.

A disadvantage of this method is that the model cannot place data in other groups than those discovered during the learning process. It is therefore very important that the training basis is representative.

Reinforcement learning

This form of learning is based on trial and error, as well as on optimisation, as the model learns which actions are targeted towards the goal. This means that less data, or no data at all, is needed for the system to learn

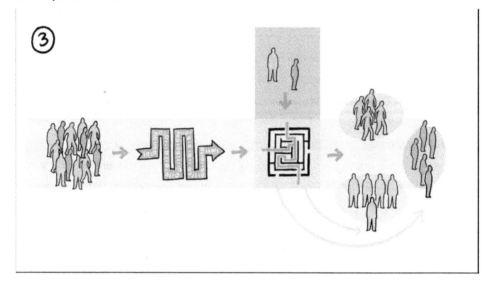

Results of learning

Regardless of the algorithms or methods used for machine learning, the result will be a "model", which is in fact an umbrella term for all machine learning. The model can then be fed with new data to produce the desired type of result. This may be, for example, a labelling, or a degree of probability, or similar.

It is worth noting that the model does not normally hold the source data directly. It holds an aggregate representation of all the data used to train the system.

Decision trees represent one exception to this, as they contain a varying degree of the model's data basis. The limits here depend on whether the tree is "pruned" after learning, or a level limitation is set for learning. One or the other will normally be chosen, as the model should generalise and not overfit. In a deep-learning model, the basic data will be represented as numerical values in the neural network. It should, therefore, not be possible to retrieve any personal data used to train the model. We shall take a closer look at these models a little later, in the section entitled the Black Box.

Model use – static and dynamic (offline/online)

A model may be used in two ways. The first way is to use a **static, or offline model**, that will not change through use. A static model will always, as the name suggests, operate in the same way and produce the same results throughout its entire lifecycle. All new model training will take place in a test environment, and all changes require that the model is replaced by a new version. This means that full control is maintained of the model in use.

The other possibility is provided by a **dynamic, or online model**. The model is used in a similar fashion to the static model. However, the difference is that the dynamic model is able to avail itself of input data in order to improve and adjust to changes. This may, for example, be necessary in connection with the monitoring of credit card transactions in order to reveal fraud. The transactions may change according to the user's life situation, or in relation to his job, by for example taking place in completely new locations. These new usage patterns could well be labelled suspicious by a static model and potentially result in a blocked credit card. A model can therefore become less accurate over time if it is not continuously updated.

A spam filter provides a good example of a typical area of application for a dynamic model which can be improved by the user indicating emails that have been wrongly labelled. The disadvantage of dynamic models is that there is less control over the model's development and the changes have immediate effect. A good example of this is the Microsoft chatbot Tay which learned from conversations with Internet users. After a brief period on Twitter the chatbot was described as a "Hitler-loving sex robot" by the media. Microsoft decided to remove Tay only 24 hours after it had been launched.

Chapter Four: Google DeepMind Learning

Illustration of the DNC architecture

(Tech Xplore)—A team of researchers at Google's DeepMind Technologies has been working on a means to increase the capabilities of computers by combining aspects of data processing and artificial intelligence and have come up with what they are calling a differentiable neural computer (DNC.) In their paper published in the journal *Nature*, they describe the work they are doing and where they believe it is headed. To make the work more accessible to the public team members, Alexander Graves and Greg Wayne have posted an explanatory page on the DeepMind website. DeepMind is a Google-owned company that does research on artificial intelligence, including neural networks, and more recently, deep neural networks, which are computer systems that learn how to do things by seeing many other examples. But, as Graves and Wayne note, such systems are typically limited by their ability to use and manipulate memory in useful ways because they are in essence based on decision trees. The work being done with DNCs is meant to overcome that deficiency, allowing for the creation of computer systems that are not only able to learn, but which will be able to remember what they have learned and then to use that information for decision making when faced with a new task. The researchers highlight an example of how such a system might be of greater use to human operators—a DNC could be taught how to get from one point to another, for example, and then caused to remember what it learned along the way. That would allow for the creation of a system that offers the best route to take on the subway, perhaps, or on a grander scale, advice on adding roads to a city.

By adding memory access to neural networking, the researchers are also looking to take advantage of another ability we humans take for granted—forming relationships between memories, particularly as they relate to time. One example would be when a person walks by a candy store and the aroma immediately takes them back to their childhood—to Christmas, perhaps, and the emotions that surround the holiday season. A computer able to make the same sorts of connections would be able to make similar leaps, jumping back to a sequence of connected learning events that could be useful in providing an answer to a problem about a certain topic—such as what caused the Great Depression or how Google became so successful.

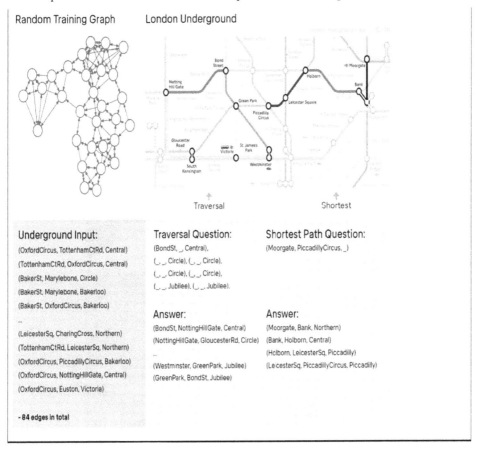

The research team has not yet revealed if there are any plans in place for actually using the systems they are developing, but it would seem likely, and it might be gradual, showing up in better search results when using Google, for example.

Artificial neural networks are remarkably adept at sensory processing, sequence learning and reinforcement learning, but are limited in their ability to represent variables and data structures and to store data over long timescales, owing to the lack of an external memory. Here we introduce a machine learning model called a differentiable neural computer (DNC), which consists of a neural network that can read from and write to an external memory matrix, analogous to the random-access memory in a conventional computer. Like a conventional computer, it can use its memory to represent and manipulate complex data structures, but, like a neural network, it can learn to do so from data. When trained with supervised learning, we demonstrate that a DNC can successfully answer synthetic questions designed to emulate reasoning and inference problems in natural language. We show that it can learn tasks such as finding the shortest path between specified points and inferring the missing links in randomly generated graphs, and then generalize these tasks to specific graphs such as transport networks and family trees. When trained with reinforcement learning, a DNC can complete a moving blocks puzzle in which changing goals are specified by sequences of symbols. Taken together, our results demonstrate that DNCs have the capacity to solve complex, structured tasks that are inaccessible to neural networks without external read–write memory.

Chapter Five: DeepMind Learning Modeling

Abstract

Since 2010 Google & Uber researchers and engineers are engaged in DeepMind project with registered company in UK and USA DeepMind. Google used to "Deep reinforcement learning" to implement DeepMind technology. We can see the results of DeepMind learning with live examples of Google Assistance, Google Echo- Smart Speaker and Google home assistance, Google AI-God and AI Church, Amazon Alexa, Amazon echo, Apple Siri. Google is one the strong player in DeepMind learning technology but two major players also Amazon and Apple after Google. This technology bring next wave in future about to 2029 but also spoiling human ethics when AI became more then of human intelligence. This short communication discussed fundamental aspect related to DeepMind designing and engineering with the help of model.

Keywords: DeepMind, Super-AI, Ultra-AI, Bionic Brain.

Introduction

DeepMind learning is the technology shift more than of AI because AI is Pre-programmed intelligence whereas DeepMind technology learn and programitself by experiences acquiring from environment and update its knowledge like human brain with more than faster of human brain.DeepMind learning is AI Deep enforcement to engineer Super-AI or Ultra-AI. Bionic Brain and Humanoid are the outstanding and breakthrough example of it. This paper shows the lucid model which assist to new entrants in the field of DeepMind and DeepMind learning. In DeepMind learning technically uses deep learning on a convolutional neural network.

Modeling

DeepMind Learning Engineering Model (DLEM)

Below figure exhibits DLEM with further discussion of all its levels. This model segmented into two parts with equal importance as Software essential module and Hardware essential module with further segmentation into three parts of each. Both the modules and their sub-modules have further lots of depth for DeepMind engineering. Here I am not showing technical aspects in detail but would like to show direction of engineering with DLEM.

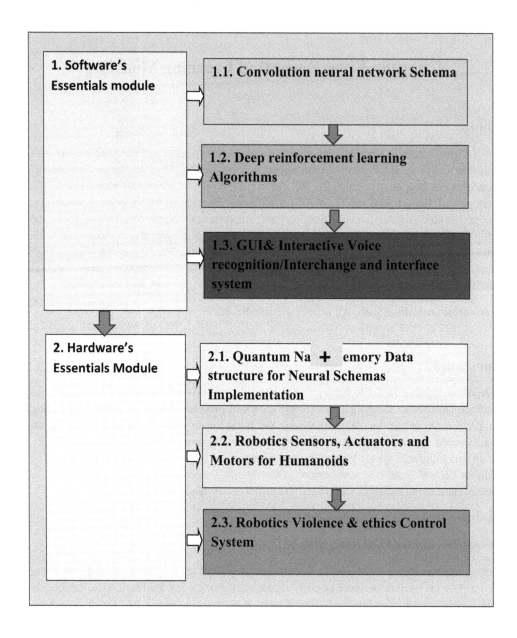

Fig: DeepMind Learning Engineering Model (DLEM)

Source: Prof.Md. Sadique Shaikh & Prof. Shabeena Khan

It clearly display in above model both modules need to engineer individually but must be full interactive and suitable to each other to show human-like or more then of Human-like intelligence with proper Avatar and appearance. Software essential module has three important engineering domains are Convolution neural network Schema, Deep reinforcement learning Algorithms , GUI & Interactive Voice recognition/Interchange and interface system and Hardware essential module has Quantum Nano Memory Data structure for Neural Schemas Implementation, Robotics Sensors, Actuators and Motors for Humanoids, Robotics Violence & ethics Control System. In Software module Convolution Neural Schemas must need to engineer those has capability and ability of self-programming and learning, at Deep enforcement learning algorithms super intelligence procedure and process design to fit in neural schemas for self learning system whereas using Human-Like GUI, Voice recognition, interaction and interchange voice command and voice response possible to/from DeepMind robots. The Second important modeling need is Hardware essential module where Quantum Nano Memory Data structure design and fabricated for Neural Schemas Implementation with ultra high processing speed this is we can say DeepMind and Neural Schemas in it make it alive with super or ultra AI can say Bionic Brain. The next phase engineering is precision sensors, actuators and motors engineering for human like movements and appearance in humanoid. The last engineering phase is most important aspect as I mentioned Google developed AI-God and Church which volatile natural beliefs of human and one day might be DeepMind AI like this made their own AI religion and ethics which would be harmful for mankind hence need to precise Robotics Violence & ethics Control System to save human from robotics violence.

Conclusion

In above communication I had discussed about DeepMind, its concepts with current examples and using Model DLEM explained how DeepMind engineering possible to carried out. I have discussed two important engineering aspects with further expansion as well also focused on how robotics violence and ethics control system is important.

Acknowledgement

I would like to credit this work to my loving wife Safeena Khan, my angel Md. Nameer Shaikh and my close friend Tanveer Sayyed as well as our Director Dr.B.N.Gupta.

References

1) Md. Sadique Shaikh, " Analysis and modeling of Strong A.I to engineer BIONIC brain for humanoid robotics application" in American Journal of Embedded System and Applications, Published by Science Publishing Group, October 2013, vol.1, No.2, doi:10.11648/ajesa.20130102.11, New York, America (U.S.A)(paper available at URL:www.sciencepublishinggroup.com/j/ajesa)

2) Md. Sadique Shaikh, "Ultra Artificial Intelligence (UAI): Redefing AI fir New Research Dimension" in Advanced Robotics & Automation (ARA), OMICS International, London, April 2017, Pgs.1-3, ISSN No: 2168-9695, Vol. 6, Issue. 2, DOI: 10.4172/2168-9695.100063. (Paper available online at URL: www.omicsonline.com

3) Md. Sadique Shaikh, "Fundamental Engineering for Brain-Computer Interfacing (BCI): Initiative for Neuron-Command Operating Devices" in Computational Biology and Bioinformatics (CBB), SciencePG, U.S.A, November 2017, Pgs. 50-56, Vol. 5, No. 4, DOI: 10.11648/j.cbb.201770504.12, (Paper available online at URL: www.sciencepublishinggroup/j/cbb)

4) Md. Sadique Shaikh, Defining ultra artificial intelligence (UAI) implementation using bionic (biological-like-electronics) brain engineering insight. *MOJ App Bio Biomech.* 2018;2(2):127–128. DOI: 10.15406/mojabb.2018.02.00054

5) MdSadiqueShaikh. Insight Artificial to Cyborg Intelligence Modeling. Arch IndEngg: 1(1): 1- 5.

6) "Artificial Intelligence Engineering for Cyborg Technology Implementation" in Robotics & Automation Engineering Journal , Robot AutomEng J. 2018; 3(1): 555604, U.S.A (Paper available at https://juniperpublishers.com/)

7) "Engineering Insight for Humanoid Robotics Emotions and Violence with Reference to "System Error 1378" in Robot AutomEng J 3(2): RAEJ.MS.ID.5555610 (2018), USA

8) "Defining Cyborg Intelligence for Medical andSuper-Human Domains" in Trends in Technical & Scientific Research, Volume 2 Issue 3 - July 2018, Trends Tech Sci Res. 2018; 2(3): 555588. Pgs. 001-002 (Available on https://juniperpublishers.com/)

9) "Ultra artificial intelligence (UAI) engineering for robotics violence control, detect and corrective measures" in International Robotics & Automation Journal, Int Rob Auto J. 2018; 4(4):242–243, DOI: 10.15406/iratj.2018.04.00129, (Available at http://medcraveonline.com)

Chapter Six: Applications and Future Perspective of DeepMind Machine Learning

Introduction

General intelligence measures an agent's ability to achieve goals in a wide range of environments (Legg and Hutter, 2007). The only known examples of general-purpose intelligence arose from a combination of evolution, development, and learning, grounded in the physics of the real world and the sensory apparatus of animals. An unknown, but potentially large, fraction of animal and human intelligence is a direct consequence of the perceptual and physical richness of our environment, and is unlikely to arise without it (e.g. Locke, 1690; Hume, 1739). One option is to directly study embodied intelligence in the real world itself using robots (e.g. Brooks, 1990; Metta et al., 2008). However, progress on that front will always be hindered by the too-slow passing of real time and the expense of the physical hardware involved. Realistic virtual worlds on the other hand, if they are sufficiently detailed, can get the best of both, combining perceptual and physical near-realism with the speed and flexibility of software.

Previous efforts to construct realistic virtual worlds as platforms for AI research have been stymied by the considerable engineering involved. To fill the gap, we present DeepMind Lab. DeepMind Lab is a first-person 3D game platform built on top of id software's Quake III Arena (id software, 1999) engine. The world is rendered with rich science fiction-style visuals. Actions are to look around and move in 3D. Example tasks include navigation in mazes, collecting fruit, traversing dangerous passages and avoiding falling off cliffs, bouncing through space using launch pads to move between platforms, laser tag, quickly learning and remembering random procedurally generated environments, and tasks inspired by Neuroscience experiments.

DeepMind Lab is already a major research platform within DeepMind. In particular, et al., 2016), unsupervised auxiliary tasks (Jaderberg et al., 2016), and to study navigation (Mirowski et al., 2016). DeepMind Lab may be compared to other game-based AI research platforms emphasising pixels-to-actions autonomous learning agents. The Arcade Learning Environment (Atari) (Bellemare et al., 2012), which we have used extensively at DeepMind, is neither 3D nor first-person. Among 3D platforms for AI research,

DeepMind Lab is comparable to others like VizDoom (Kempka et al., 2016) and Minecraft (Johnson et al., 2016; Tessler et al., 2016). However, it pushes the envelope beyond what is possible in those platforms. In comparison, DeepMind Lab has considerably richer visuals and more naturalistic physics. The action space allows for fine-grained pointing in a fully 3D world. Compared to VizDoom, DeepMind\ Lab is more removed from its origin in a first-person shooter genre video game. This work is different and complementary to other recent projects which run as plugins to access internal content in the Unreal engine (Qiu and Yuille, 2016; Lerer et al., 2016). Any of these systems can be used to generate static datasets for computer vision as described e.g., in Mahendran et al. (2016); Richter et al. (2016). Artificial general intelligence (AGI) research in DeepMind Lab emphasises 3D vision from raw pixel inputs, first-person (egocentric) viewpoints, fine motor dexterity, navigation, planning, strategy, time, and fully autonomous agents that must learn for themselves what tasks to perform by exploration of their environment. All these factors make learning difficult. Each are considered frontier research questions on their own. Putting them all together in one platform, as we have, is a significant challenge for the field.

DeepMind Lab Research Platform

DeepMind Lab is built on top of id software's Quake III Arena (id software, 1999) engine using the ioquake3 (Nussel et al., 2016) version of the codebase, which is actively maintained by enthusiasts in the open source community. DeepMind Lab also includes tools from q3map2 (GtkRadiant, 2016) and bspc (bspc, 2016) for level generation. The bot scripts are based on code from the OpenArena (OpenArena, 2016) project. Tailored for machine learning A custom set of assets were created to give the platform a unique and stylised look and feel, with a focus on rich visuals tailored for machine learning.

A reinforcement learning API has been built on top of the game engine, providing agents with complex observations and accepting a rich set of actions. The interaction with the platform is lock-stepped, with the engine stepped forward one simulation step (or multiple with repeated actions, if desired) at a time, according to a user-specified frame rate. Thus, the game is effectively paused after an observation is provided until an agent provides the next action(s) to take. Observations

At each step, the engine provides reward, pixel-based observations and, optionally, velocity information (figure 1):

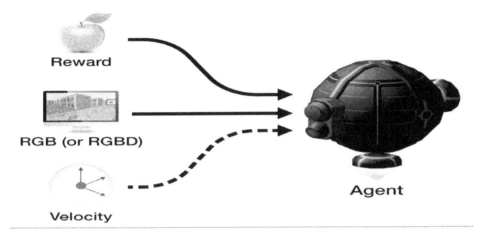

Figure 1: Observations available to the agent. In our experience, reward and pixels are sufficient to train an agent, whereas depth and velocity information can be useful for further analysis.

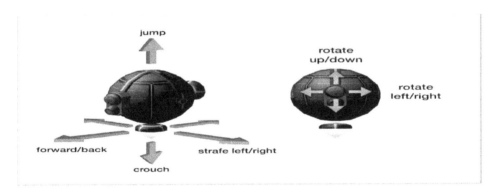

Figure 2: The action space includes movement in three dimensions and look direction around two axes.

1. The reward signal is a scalar value that is effectively the score of each level.

2. The platform provides access to the raw pixels as rendered by the game engine from the player's first-person perspective, formatted as RGB pixels. There is also an RGBD format, which

additionally exposes per-pixel depth values, mimicking the range sensors used in robotics and biological stereo-vision.

3. For certain research applications the agent's translational and angular velocities may be useful. These are exposed as two separate three-dimensional vectors.

Actions Agents can provide multiple simultaneous actions to control movement (forward/back, strafe left/right, crouch, jump), looking (up/down, left/right) and tagging (in laser tag levels with opponent bots), as illustrated in figure 2.

Example levels

Figures show a gallery of screen shots from the first-person perspective of the agent. The levels can be divided into four categories:

1. Simple fruit gathering levels with a static map (seekavoid_arena_01 and stairway_to_melon). The goal of these levels is to collect apples (small positive reward) and melons (large positive reward) while avoiding lemons (small negative reward).

2. Navigation levels with a static map layout (nav_maze_static_0f1; 2; 3g and nav_maze_random_goal_0f1; 2; 3g). These levels test the agent's ability to find their way to a goal in a fixed maze that remains the same across episodes.

The starting location is random. In the random goal variant, the location of the goal changes in every episode. The optimal policy is to find the goal's location at the start of each episode and then use long-term knowledge of the maze layout to return to it as quickly as possible from any location. The static variant is simpler in that the goal location is always fixed for all episodes and only the agent's starting location changes so the optimal policy does not require the first step of exploring to find the current goal location. The specific layouts are shown in figure 3.

3. Procedurally-generated navigation levels requiring effective exploration of a new maze generated on-the-fly at the start of each episode (random_maze). These levels test the agent's ability to explore a totally new environment. The optimal policy would begin by exploring the maze to rapidly learn its layout and then exploit that knowledge to repeatedly return to the goal as many times as possible before the end of the episode (three minutes).

4. Laser-tag levels requiring agents to wield laser-like science fiction gadgets to tag bots controlled by the game's in-built AI (lt_horseshoe_color, lt_chasm, lt_hallway_slope, and lt_space_bounce_hard). A reward of 1 is delivered whenever the agent tags a bot by reducing its

shield to 0. These levels approximate the usual gameplay from Quake III Arena. In lt_hallway_slope there is a sloped arena, requiring the agent to look up and down. In lt_chasm and lt_space_bounce_hard there are pits that the agent must jump over and avoidfalling into. In lt_horseshoe_color and lt_space_bounce_hard, the colours and textures of the bots are randomly generated at the start of each episode.

This prevents agents from relying on colour for bot detection. These levels test aspects of fine-control (for aiming), planning (to anticipate where bots are likely to move), strategy (to control key areas of the map such as gadget spawn points), and robustness to the substantial visual complexity arising from the large numbers of independently moving objects (gadget projectiles and bots).

Technical Details

The original game engine is written in C and, to ensure compatibility with future changes to the engine, it has only been modified where necessary. DeepMind Lab provides a simple C API and ships with Python bindings.

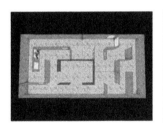

Figure 3: Top-down views of static maze levels. Left: nav_maze_static_01, middle: nav_maze_static_02 and right: nav_maze_static_03.

level creation and mechanics. This approach has resulted in a highly flexible platform with minimal changes to the original game engine.

DeepMind Lab supports Linux and has been tested on several major distributions. API for agents and humans The engine can be run either in a window, or it can be run headless for higher performance and support for non-windowed environments like a remote terminal. Rendering uses OpenGL and can make use of either a GPU or a software renderer. A DeepMind

Lab instance is initialised with the user's settings for level name, screen resolution and frame rate. After initialisation a simple RL-style API is followed to interact with the environment, as per figure 4.

Level generation

Levels for DeepMind Lab are Quake III Arena levels. They are packaged into: pk3 files (which are ZIP files) and consist of a number of components, including level geometry, navigation information and textures. DeepMind Lab includes tools to generate maps from: map files. These can be cumbersome to edit by hand, but a variety of level editors are freely available, e.g. GtkRadiant (GtkRadiant, 2016). In addition to built-in and user-provided levels, the platform offers Text Levels, which are simple, human-readable text files, to specify walls, spawn points and other game mechanics as shown in the example in figure 4. Refer to figure for a render of the generated level.

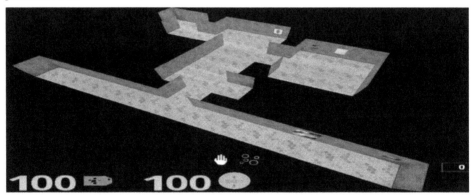

Figure 4: A level with the layout generated from the text in figure.

The brain optimizes cost functions

The central hypothesis for linking the two fields is that biological systems, like many machine learning systems, are able to optimize cost functions. The idea of cost functions means that neurons in a brain area can somehow change their properties, e.g., the properties of their synapses, so that they get better at doing whatever the cost function dense as their role. Human behavior sometimes approaches optimality in a domain, e.g., during movement (Kording, 2007), which suggests that the brain may have learned optimal strategies. Subjects minimize energy consumption of their movement system (Taylor and Faisal, 2011), and minimize risk and damage to their body, while maximizing financial and movement gains. Computationally, we now know that optimization of trajectories gives rise to elegant solutions for very complex motor tasks (Mordatch et al., 2012; Todorov and Jordan, 2002; Harris and Wolpert, 1998). We suggest that cost function optimization occurs much more generally in shaping the internal representations and processes used by the brain. We also suggest that this requires the brain to have mechanisms for efficient credit assignment in multilayer and recurrent networks

Cost functions are diverse across areas and change over development

A second realization is that cost functions need not be global. Neurons in deferent brain areas may optimize deferent things, e.g., the mean squared error of movements, surprise in a visual stimulus, or the allocation of attention. Importantly, such a cost function could be locally generated. For example, neurons could locally evaluate the quality of their statistical model of their inputs (Figure 1B). Alternatively, cost functions for one area could be generated by another area. Moreover, cost functions may change over time, e.g., guiding young humans to understanding simple visual contrasts early on, and faces a bit later. This could allow the developing brain to bootstrap more complex knowledge based on simpler knowledge. Cost functions in the brain are likely to be complex and to be arranged to vary across areas and over development.

Specialized systems allow efficiently solving key computational problems

A third realization is that structure matters. The patterns of information own seem fundamentally deferent across brain areas, suggesting that they solve distinct computational problems.

Some brain areas are highly recurrent, perhaps making them predestined for short-term memory storage (Wang, 2012). Some areas contain cell types that can switch between qualitatively deferent states of activation, such as a persistent during mode versus a transient during mode, in response to particular neurotransmitters (Hasselmo, 2006). Other areas, like the thalamus appear to have the information from other areas owing through them, perhaps allowing them to determine information routing (Sherman, 2005).

Areas like the basal ganglia are involved in reinforcement learning and gating of discrete decisions (Sejnowski and Poizner, 2014; Doya, 1999). As every programmer knows, specialized algorithms matter for efficient solutions to computational problems, and the brain is likely to make good use of such specialization (Figure 1C). These ideas are inspired by recent advances in machine learning, but we also propose that the brain has major differences from any of today's machine learning techniques. In particular, the world gives us a relatively limited amount of information that we could use for supervised learning (Fodor and Crowther, 2002). There is a huge amount of information available for unsupervised learning, but there is no reason to assume that a generic unsupervised algorithm, no matter how powerful, would learn the precise things that humans need to know, in the order that they need to know it. The evolutionary challenge of making unsupervised learning solve the right" problems is, therefore, to end a sequence of cost functions that will deterministically build circuits and behaviors according to prescribed developmental stages, so that in the end a relatively small amount of information success to produce the right behavior. For example, a developing duck imprints (Tinbergen, 1965) a template of its parent, and then uses that template to generate goal-targets that help it develop other skills like foraging. Generalizing from this and from other studies (Ullman et al., 2012; Minsky, 1977), we propose that many of the brain's cost functions arise from such an internal bootstrapping process. Indeed, we propose that biological development and reinforcement learning can, in effect, program the emergence of a sequence of cost functions that precisely anticipates the future needs faced by the brain's internal subsystems, as well as by the organism as a whole. This type of developmentally programmed bootstrapping generates an internal infrastructure of cost functions which is diverse and complex, while simplifying the learning problems faced by the brain's internal processes.

Beyond simple tasks like familial imprinting, this type of bootstrapping could extend to higher cognition, e.g., internally generated cost functions could train a developing brain to properly access its memory or to organize its actions in ways that will prove to be useful later on. The potential bootstrapping mechanisms that we will consider operate in the context of unsupervised and reinforcement learning, and go well beyond the types of curriculum learning ideas used in today's machine learning (Bengio et al., 2009).

In the rest of this paper, we will elaborate on these hypotheses. First, we will argue that both local and multi-layer optimization is, perhaps surprisingly, compatible with what we know about the brain. Second, we will argue that cost functions differ across brain areas and change over time and describe how cost functions interacting in an orchestrated way could allow bootstrapping of complex function. Third, we will list a broad set of specialized problems that need to be solved by neural computation, and the brain areas that have structure that seems to be matched to a particular computational problem.

We then discuss some implications of the above hypotheses for research approaches in neuroscience and machine learning, and sketch a set of experiments to test these hypotheses. Finally, we discuss this architecture from the perspective of evolution.

The brain can optimize cost functions

Much of machine learning is based on efficiently optimizing functions, and, as we will detail below, the ability to use back propagation of error (Werbos, 1974; Rumelhart et al., 1986) to calculate gradients of arbitrary parametrized functions has been a key breakthrough. In Hypothesis 1, we claim that the brain is also, at least in part, an optimization machine. But what exactly does it mean to say that the brain can optimize cost functions? After all, many processes can be viewed as optimizations. For example, the laws of physics are often viewed as minimizing an action functional, while evolution optimizes the fitness of replicators over a long timescale. To be clear, our main claims are: that a) the brain has powerful mechanisms for credit assignment during learning that allow it to optimize global functions in multi-layer networks by adjusting the properties of each neuron to contribute to the global outcome, and that b) the brain has mechanisms to specify exactly which cost functions it subjects its networks to, i.e., that the cost functions are highly tunable, shaped by evolution and matched to the animal's ethological needs. Thus, the brain uses cost functions as a key driving force of its development, much as modern machine learning systems do.

To understand the basis of these claims, we must now delve into the details of how the brain might efficiently perform credit assignment throughout large, multi-layered networks, in order to optimize complex functions. We argue that the brain uses several different types of optimization to solve distinct problems. In some structures, it may use genetic pre-specification of circuits for problems that require only limited learning based on data, or it may exploit local optimization to avoid the need to assign credit through many layers of neurons. It may also use a host of proposed circuit structures that would allow it to actually perform, in effect, back propagation of errors through a multi-layer network, using biologically realistic mechanisms { a feat that had once been widely believed to be biologically implausible (Crick, 1989; Stork, 1989). Potential such mechanisms include circuits that literally back propagate error derivatives in the manner of conventional back propagation, as well as circuits that provide other efficient means of approximating the effects of back propagation, i.e., of rapidly computing the approximate gradient of a cost function relative to any given connection weight in the network. Lastly, the brain may use algorithms that exploit specific aspects of neurophysiology { such as spike timing dependent plasticity, dendritic computation, local excitatory-inhibitory networks, or other properties { as well as the integrated nature of higher-level brain systems. Such mechanisms promise to allow learning capabilities that go even beyond those of current back propagation networks.

A) In conventional deep learning, supervised training is based on externally-supplied, labeled data.

B) In the brain, supervised training of networks can still occur via gradient descent on an error signal, but this error signal must arise from internally generated cost functions. These cost functions are themselves computed by neural modules specified by both genetics and learning. Internally generated cost functions create heuristics that are used to bootstrap more complex learning. For example, an area which recognizes faces might _rst be trained to detect faces using simple heuristics, like the presence of two dots above a line, and then further trained to discriminate salient facial expressions using representations arising from unsupervised learning and error signals from other brain areas related to social reward processing.

C) Internally generated cost functions and error-driven training of cortical deep networks form part of a larger architecture containing several specialized systems. Although the trainable cortical areas are schematized as feed forward neural networks here, LSTMs or other types of recurrent networks may be a more accurate analogy, and many neuronal properties such as spiking, dendritic computation, neuro-modulation, adaptation, timing-dependent plasticity, direct electrical connections, transient synaptic dynamics, spontaneous activity, and others, will inuence what and how such networks learn.

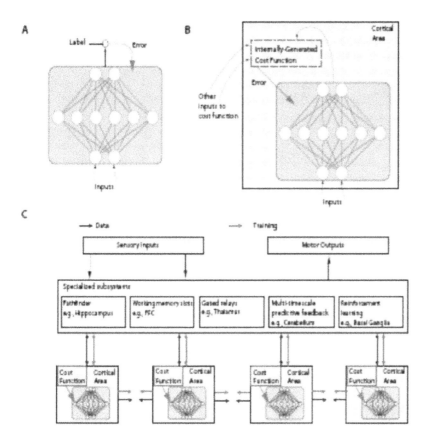

Fig 1: Putative differences between conventional and brain-like neural network designs.

References

Marc G Bellemare, Yavar Naddaf, Joel Veness, and Michael Bowling. The arcade learning environment: An evaluation platform for general agents. Journal of Artificial Intelligence Research, 2012. Rodney A Brooks. Elephants don't play chess. Robotics and autonomous systems, 6
(1):3–15, 1990.

bspc. bspc, 2016. URL https://github.com/TTimo/bspc.

GtkRadiant. Gtkradiant, 2016. URL http://icculus.org/gtkradiant/.

David Hume. Treatise on human nature. 1739. id software. Quake3, 1999. URL https://github.com/id-Software/Quake-III-Arena.

Max Jaderberg, Volodymyr Mnih, Wojciech Marian Czarnecki, Tom Schaul, Joel Z Leibo, David Silver, and Koray Kavukcuoglu. Reinforcement learning with unsupervised auxiliary tasks. arXiv preprint arXiv:1611.05397, 2016.

Matthew Johnson, Katja Hofmann, Tim Hutton, and David Bignell. The malmo platform for artificial intelligence experimentation. In International joint conference on artificial intelligence (IJCAI), 2016.

Michał Kempka, Marek Wydmuch, Grzegorz Runc, Jakub Toczek, and Wojciech Jaskowski. Vizdoom: A doom-based ai research platform for visual reinforcement learning. arXiv preprint arXiv:1605.02097, 2016.

Shane Legg and Marcus Hutter. Universal intelligence: A definition of machine intelligence. Minds and Machines, 17(4):391–444, 2007.

Adam Lerer, Sam Gross, and Rob Fergus. Learning physical intuition of block towers by example. arXiv preprint arXiv:1603.01312, 2016.

John Locke. An essay concerning human understanding. 1690.
A Mahendran, H Bilen, JF Henriques, and A Vedaldi. Researchdoom and cocodoom: Learning computer vision with games. arXiv preprint arXiv:1610.02431, 2016.

Giorgio Metta, Giulio Sandini, David Vernon, Lorenzo Natale, and Francesco Nori. The icub humanoid robot: an open platform for research in embodied cognition. In Proceedings of the 8th workshop on performance metrics for intelligent systems, pages 50–56. ACM, 2008.

Piotr Mirowski, Razvan Pascanu, Fabio Viola, Hubert Soyer, Andy Ballard, Andrea Banino, Misha Denil, Ross Goroshin, Laurent Sifre, Koray Kavukcuoglu, et al. Learning to navigate in complex environments. arXiv preprint arXiv:1611.03673, 2016.

Volodymyr Mnih, Adria Puigdomenech Badia, Mehdi Mirza, Alex Graves, Timothy P Lillicrap, Tim Harley, David Silver, and Koray Kavukcuoglu. Asynchronous methods for deep reinforcement learning. arXiv preprint arXiv:1602.01783, 2016.

Ludwig Nussel, Thilo Schulz, Tim Angus, Tony J White, and Zachary J Slater. ioquake3, 2016. URL https://github.com/ioquake/ioq3.

OpenArena. The openarena project, 2016. URL http://www.openarena.ws.

Weichao Qiu and Alan Yuille. Unrealcv: Connecting computer vision to unreal engine. arXiv preprint arXiv:1609.01326, 2016.

Stephan R Richter, Vibhav Vineet, Stefan Roth, and Vladlen Koltun. Playing for data: Ground truth from computer games. In European Conference on Computer

Vision, pages 102–118. Springer, 2016.

Chen Tessler, Shahar Givony, Tom Zahavy, Daniel J Mankowitz, and Shie Mannor.
A deep hierarchical approach to lifelong learning in minecraft. arXiv preprint
arXiv:1604.07255, 2016.

Leemon Baird. Residual algorithms: Reinforcement learning with function approximation. In
Proceedings of the 12th International Conference on Machine Learning (ICML 1995), pages
30–37. Morgan Kaufmann, 1995.

Marc Bellemare, Joel Veness, and Michael Bowling. Sketch-based linear value function
approximation.
In Advances in Neural Information Processing Systems 25, pages 2222–2230,
2012.

Marc G Bellemare, Yavar Naddaf, Joel Veness, and Michael Bowling. The arcade learning
environment: An evaluation platform for general agents. Journal of Artificial Intelligence
Research, 47:253–279, 2013.

Marc G Bellemare, Joel Veness, and Michael Bowling. Investigating contingency awareness
using atari 2600 games. In AAAI, 2012.

Marc G. Bellemare, Joel Veness, and Michael Bowling. Bayesian learning of recursively
factored environments. In Proceedings of the Thirtieth International Conference on Machine
Learning (ICML 2013), pages 1211–1219, 2013.

George E. Dahl, Dong Yu, Li Deng, and Alex Acero. Context-dependent pre-trained deep
neural networks for large-vocabulary speech recognition. Audio, Speech, and Language
Processing, IEEE Transactions on, 20(1):30 –42, January 2012.

Alex Graves, Abdel-rahman Mohamed, and Geoffrey E. Hinton. Speech recognition with deep recurrent neural networks. In Proc. ICASSP, 2013.

Matthew Hausknecht, Risto Miikkulainen, and Peter Stone. A neuro-evolution approach to general atari game playing. 2013.

Nicolas Heess, David Silver, and Yee Whye Teh. Actor-critic reinforcement learning with energy-based policies. In European Workshop on Reinforcement Learning, page 43, 2012.

Kevin Jarrett, Koray Kavukcuoglu, MarcAurelio Ranzato, and Yann LeCun. What is the best multi-stage architecture for object recognition? In Proc. International Conference on Computer Vision and Pattern Recognition (CVPR 2009), pages 2146–2153. IEEE, 2009.

Alex Krizhevsky, Ilya Sutskever, and Geoff Hinton. Imagenet classification with deep convolutional neural networks. In Advances in Neural Information Processing Systems 25, pages 1106–1114, 2012.

Sascha Lange and Martin Riedmiller. Deep auto-encoder neural networks in reinforcement learning. In Neural Networks (IJCNN), The 2010 International Joint Conference on, pages 1–8. IEEE, 2010.

Long-Ji Lin. Reinforcement learning for robots using neural networks. Technical report, DTIC Document, 1993.

Hamid Maei, Csaba Szepesvari, Shalabh Bhatnagar, Doina Precup, David Silver, and Rich Sutton. Convergent Temporal-Difference Learning with Arbitrary Smooth Function Approximation. In Advances in Neural Information Processing Systems 22, pages 1204–1212, 2009.

Hamid Maei, Csaba Szepesv´ari, Shalabh Bhatnagar, and Richard S. Sutton. Toward off-policy learning control with function approximation. In Proceedings of the 27th International Conference on Machine Learning (ICML 2010), pages 719–726, 2010.

Volodymyr Mnih. Machine Learning for Aerial Image Labeling. PhD thesis, University of Toronto, 2013. Andrew Moore and Chris Atkeson. Prioritized sweeping: Reinforcement learning with less data and less real time. Machine Learning, 13:103–130, 1993.

Vinod Nair and Geoffrey E Hinton. Rectified linear units improve restricted boltzmann machines. In Proceedings of the 27th International Conference on Machine Learning (ICML 2010), pages 807–814, 2010.

Jordan B. Pollack and Alan D. Blair. Why did td-gammon work. In Advances in Neural Information Processing Systems 9, pages 10–16, 1996.

Martin Riedmiller. Neural fitted q iteration–first experiences with a data efficient neural reinforcement learning method. In Machine Learning: ECML 2005, pages 317–328. Springer, 2005.

Brian Sallans and Geoffrey E. Hinton. Reinforcement learning with factored states and actions. Journal of Machine Learning Research, 5:1063–1088, 2004.

Pierre Sermanet, Koray Kavukcuoglu, Soumith Chintala, and Yann LeCun. Pedestrian detection with unsupervised multi-stage feature learning. In Proc. International Conference on Computer Vision and Pattern Recognition (CVPR 2013). IEEE, 2013.

Richard Sutton and Andrew Barto. Reinforcement Learning: An Introduction. MIT Press, 1998. Gerald Tesauro. Temporal difference learning and td-gammon. Communications of the ACM, 38(3):58–68, 1995.

John N Tsitsiklis and Benjamin Van Roy. An analysis of temporal-difference learning with function approximation. Automatic Control, IEEE Transactions on, 42(5):674–690, 1997. Christopher JCH Watkins and Peter Dayan. Q-learning. Machine learning, 8(3-4):279–292, 1992.

Publisher: Eliva Press SRL

Email: info@elivapress.com

Eliva Press is an independent publishing house established for the publication and dissemination of academic works all over the world. Company provides high quality and professional service for all of our authors.

Our Services:
Free of charge, open-minded, eco-friendly, innovational.

-Free standard publishing services (manuscript review, step-by-step book preparation, publication, distribution, and marketing).
-No financial risk. The author is not obliged to pay any hidden fees for publication.
-Editors. Dedicated editors will assist step by step through the projects.
-Money paid to the author for every book sold. Up to 50% royalties guaranteed.
-ISBN (International Standard Book Number). We assign a unique ISBN to every Eliva Press book.
-Digital archive storage. Books will be available online for a long time. We don't need to have a stock of our titles. No unsold copies. Eliva Press uses environment friendly print on demand technology that limits the needs of publishing business. We care about environment and share these principles with our customers.
-Cover design. Cover art is designed by a professional designer.
-Worldwide distribution. We continue expanding our distribution channels to make sure that all readers have access to our books.

www.elivapress.com